FORMALDEHYDE - An Assessment of Its Health Effects

prepared for the

Consumer Product Safety Commission

by the

COMMITTEE ON TOXICOLOGY

Board on Toxicology and Environmental Health Hazards
Assembly of Life Sciences
National Research Council

NATIONAL ACADEMY OF SCIENCES
Washington, D.C.

March 1980

NOTICE

The project that is the subject of this report was approved by the Governing Board of the National Research Council, whose members are drawn from the Councils of the National Academy of Sciences, the National Academy of Engineering, and the Institute of Medicine. The members of the Committee responsible for the report were chosen for their special competences and with regard for appropriate balance.

This report has been reviewed by a group other than the authors according to procedures approved by a Report Review Committee consisting of members of the National Academy of Sciences, the National Academy of Engineering, and the Institute of Medicine.

This report was prepared under Contract N00014-79-C-0049 between the National Academy of Sciences and the Office of Naval Research.

COMMITTEE ON TOXICOLOGY

Joseph F. Borzelleca, Virginia Commonwealth University, Chairman
David Axelrod, New York State Health Department
Lawrence Fishbein, National Center for Toxicological Research
Ian T. Higgins, University of Michigan Medical Center
Wendell W. Kilgore, University of California-Davis
Howard I. Maibach, University of California-San Francisco
H. George Mandel, George Washington University School of Medicine
Roger O. McClellan, Lovelace Biomedical and Environmental Research Institute
Charles F. Reinhardt, E.I. duPont de Nemours and Company
Joseph V. Rodricks, Food and Drug Administration
Ronald C. Shank, University of California-Irvine
Carl M. Shy, University of North Carolina at Chapel Hill
Peter Spencer, Albert Einstein College of Medicine
Philip G. Watanabe, Dow Chemical U.S.A.

Staff Scientists: Gary R. Keilson
                    Gordon W. Newell

The Committee on Toxicology would like to acknowledge the support of Dr. Joel Bender for assistance in preparation of the report, Mr. Norman Grossblatt for editing the report, Miss Virginia White and Mrs. Edna Paulson for preparation and verification of the references, and Ms. Brenda Spears and Mrs. Beulah Bresler for their invaluable assistance in preparation of the manuscripts.

CONTENTS

	Page
PREFACE	iv
EXECUTIVE SUMMARY	v
INTRODUCTION	1
PUBLIC EXPOSURE	1
EFFECTS ON ANIMALS	4
Short-Term Studies	4
Prolonged Studies	5
Carcinogenic Potential	6
Mutagenic Potential	8
Embryotoxic/Teratogenic Potential	8
EFFECTS ON HUMANS	9
Controlled Experiments With Airborne Formaldehyde	9
Physiologic Endpoints	10
SUMMARY OF ANIMAL AND HUMAN EXPOSURE TO FORMALDEHYDE	13
Animal Exposure	13
Human Exposure	13
ANALYTICAL METHODS	14
INHALATION EXPOSURE LIMITS	14
COMMITTEE SUMMARY AND RECOMMENDATIONS	15
Summary	15
Recommendations	17
TABLES	20
REFERENCES	30

PREFACE

It must be recognized that the concerns and deliberations that led to development of this document have to a certain extent been superseded by the recent preliminary report from the Chemical Industry Institute of Toxicology (CIIT), which indicated that formaldehyde exposure induced nasopharyngeal carcinoma in rats.

It is strongly recommended that, when the CIIT study has been reported in detail and the results are available for evaluation, an appropriate peer group should review and comment on the investigation. Thus, this presentation should be considered only an interim report on the health effects of formaldehyde.

EXECUTIVE SUMMARY

The Consumer Product Safety Commission (CPSC) and various state health agencies have received over 500 complaints from consumers, primarily related to eye and upper respiratory tract irritation. The source of these problems appeared to be the offgassing of formaldehyde from urea-formaldehyde foam insulation, particle board, or plywood. As a result, the CPSC requested the Committee on Toxicology to review and evaluate the formaldehyde literature in order to determine whether a tolerable concentration of airborne formaldehyde could be recommended for long-term continuous exposure in the household environment.

Formaldehyde is widely used, both by itself and as a constituent in other products. Public exposure in indoor air can result from a number of sources, including cigarette smoke, formaldehyde-containing resinous products, and cooking. Several investigators evaluated the health effects of formaldehyde in indoor air reported by consumers over a wide range of concentrations, from 0.01 to 31.7 ppm. The predominant symptoms were eye and upper respiratory tract irritation, headaches, drowsiness, and gastrointestinal disturbances. Effects reported at very low airborne concentrations suggest the existence of a hypersensitive group within the population. However, because the investigations studied only the individuals who complained of health effects, the size of the hypersensitive population could not be identified. In addition, other pollutants are present in the home, and the contribution of formaldehyde to the overall health effects has yet to be ascertained. Studies of airborne formaldehyde in the workplace and in controlled exposures also indicate that the eyes, respiratory tract, and skin are the organ systems predominantly affected. These latter investigations, particularly the controlled exposures, provided the best dose-response data on the irritancy of formaldehyde at low airborne concentrations.

Formaldehyde has been investigated in animals for short periods, as well as for more prolonged exposures. These studies have demonstrated the irritating properties of formaldehyde to body tissues and its effects on pulmonary function, over a wide range of concentrations. However, they have not provided a delineation of the effects to the eye and upper respiratory tract that were reported in the household environment at low airborne concentrations.

An ongoing lifetime inhalation study in rats and mice has indicated that there may be a carcinogenic effect of exposure to formaldehyde. There is a high incidence of squamous cell carcinoma in the nasomaxillary epithelium of rats exposed to formaldehyde at 15 ppm, 6 h/d, 5 d/wk for 18 mo, with histologic changes in the nasal epithelium of rats at 6 and 2 ppm. Similar results have not been reported for mice exposed at the same concentrations. Because these results reflect only interim findings, and the study has yet to be subject to independent peer review, the Committee did not incorporate the findings into its assessment of the health risks of formaldehyde. The CPSC, however, is urged to have the completed study reviewed by an independent body, for an estimate of the carcinogenic potential of formaldehyde to humans.

Formaldehyde has been shown to be mutagenic in several nonmammalian test systems, such as microorganisms and insects, but was negative in the Ames test and there have been conflicting findings in mammalian test systems. Such equivocal results demonstrate the need for additional studies to clarify the mutagenic potential of this compound in mammalian cells.

On the basis of available data, the Committee concludes that there is no population threshold for the irritant effects of formaldehyde in humans. Information from controlled human studies and complaint-related investigations suggests that, even at extremely low airborne concentrations, a proportion of the population will respond with some irritation. The Committee provides a range of irritation responses associated with exposure to formaldehyde. This tabulation was developed from the controlled human studies, which provide the only data on the extent of irritation caused by exposure at low airborne concentrations. The Committee recognizes that the general population may react with greater frequency and severity than these test populations; however, no realistic estimate of the magnitude of this effect is possible with the current and limited data.

During the course of this investigation, it became evident that certain research was necessary if the health risks associated with formaldehyde were to be assessed fully. In this regard, the CPSC is urged to pursue the research agenda outlined in this document.

At present, the irritant effects appear to be the most sensitive responses from exposure to formaldehyde. However, identification of the toxicologic reaction of greatest concern to man must await conclusion of ongoing and planned studies. Because of this uncertainty and because of the unresolved issues surrounding the carcinogenicity of formaldehyde, the extent of variability of responses in normal populations and in hypersensitive groups, and the population threshold for irritant effects, the Committee recommends that formaldehyde be kept at the lowest practical concentration in indoor residential air. In the selection of such a concentration, several issues must be taken into consideration, including a judgment of acceptable degrees of risk and response, economic impacts, sensitivity of analytical methods, and background outdoor-air concentrations.

INTRODUCTION

Over the last few years, the Consumer Product Safety Commission (CPSC) has received complaints from individuals who experienced a variety of adverse health effects reportedly associated with exposure to formaldehyde, including upper respiratory tract and eye irritation, headaches, nosebleeds, and gastrointestinal symptoms. As a result, the CPSC has asked the National Research Council's Committee on Toxicology to evaluate the pertinent literature on the toxicity of formaldehyde and to consider whether a tolerable concentration of airborne formaldehyde can be recommended for long-term continuous exposure in the household environment.

In its pure form, formaldehyde is a colorless gas with a pungent odor. An American Chemical Society monograph on formaldehyde includes a comprehensive discussion of its physical and chemical properties (Walker, 1964). Formaldehyde has high chemical reactivity, good thermal stability, and readily polymerizes; all of these characteristics make it a useful material in the synthesis of a wide variety of products. Aqueous solutions are the most common form of formaldehyde, although alcohol solutions are also available. Formalin is an aqueous solution with a formaldehyde content of 37-50%, by weight. These solutions may contain stabilizers to inhibit polymer formation. Methanol is most often used for this purpose, at concentrations of 10-15% by weight. Paraformaldehyde, a solid polymer of formaldehyde, can be vaporized to its monomeric form, which makes it a useful material as a source of formaldehyde in laboratory experiments.

Several billion pounds of formaldehyde are produced each year in the United States. Its reactions with amino acids, proteins, and nucleic acids are important in yielding protein denaturants for use in leather tanning, as preservatives, and in the preparation of vaccines. It is widely used in the manufacture of phenolic, urea, and melamine resins. These materials are used in bonding particle board, in laminating veneers and plywood, and as insulating materials, dinnerware, protective coatings, and special treatments for textiles and paper products.

Under certain conditions, formaldehyde is released from resinous products by diffusion, decomposition, or environmental degradation. Products known to release formaldehyde over a prolonged period include urea-formaldehyde foam insulation, particle board, and plywood. The consumer may also encounter formaldehyde in pesticides, cosmetics, and pharmaceuticals.

This report deals with the effects of formaldehyde on animals, humans, and in *in vitro* tests. The Committee conducted an extensive search of the literature on formaldehyde. From a review of several hundred references, it selected material pertinent to an assessment of the health risks associated with exposure to airborne formaldehyde. For more details and inclusive surveys of potential health effects, the reader is referred to several reviews on this subject (Battelle Columbus Laboratories, 1977b; CIIT, 1979a; Loomis, 1979; NRC, [1980]; USDHEW, 1976a).

PUBLIC EXPOSURE

Formaldehyde emissions from industrial processes are generally confined to the immediate vicinity of the plant. Primary sources of potential public exposure include cigarette smoke, automotive exhaust, photochemical smog, incinerators, and degassing of urea-formaldehyde resinous products.

Formaldehyde in outdoor air can derive from a number of sources. Incomplete combustion of hydrocarbons accounts for much of the formaldehyde present in the atmosphere. Automotive exhausts have been reported to contain formaldehyde at 29-43 ppm (Altshuller et al., 1961). Approximately 6 pounds of formaldehyde is produced during combustion of 1,000 pounds of gasoline (Kitchens et al., 1976). Mobile sources (automobiles, diesel engines, and aircraft engines) emit about 666 million pounds of formaldehyde annually. Local concentrations may vary with traffic patterns and vehicular density.

Municipal incinerators emit about 0.6-0.9 pounds of formaldehyde per ton of refuse, or 13.1 million pounds of formaldehyde annually (Kitchens et al., 1976). Ground level air concentrations of 0.1 ppb have been projected from incinerator emissions (Battelle Columbus Laboratories, 1977b). Experimental incinerator exhaust contains formaldehyde at 0.1-1 ppm (Altshuller et al. 1961). Stationary and mobile combustion sources emit about 840 million pounds of formaldehyde a year (Kitchens et al., 1976).

Photochemical smog can be an important source of formaldehyde. Stupfel (1976) reported that outdoor air in Los Angeles contained formaldehyde at 0.05-0.12 ppm over the course of 26 days of measurements. Measurements taken during the fall of 1961 averaged 0.04 ppm, with an average daily maximum of 0.06 ppm (Altshuller and McPherson, 1963). Approximately 13% of the daily maximums exceeded 0.1 ppm. The highest measured concentration was 0.16 ppm. More recent measurements of outdoor air in Mission Viejo, California indicated average concentrations of total aldehydes (as formaldehyde) of 0.014 ppm (Hollowell et al., 1979a). At a research facility in Ames, Iowa, outdoor formaldehyde concentrations were below 0.005 ppm (Hollowell et al., 1979a).

A heavy smoker can be exposed to a considerable amount of formaldehyde. Cigarette smoke contains as much as 40 ppm of formaldehyde by volume (Battelle Columbus Laboratories, 1977b; Kensler and Battista, 1963). With 95% retention from 10 40-ml puffs on each of 20 cigarettes, a smoker could receive a total daily burden of 0.38 mg of formaldehyde. It has also been reported that, when 5 cigarettes were smoked in a 30-m^3 climatic chamber, the concentration of formaldehyde reached 0.23 ppm; acrolein and carbon monoxide were present at 0.05 and 12 ppm, respectively (Weber-Tschopp et al., 1976). Other potential sources of formaldehyde in the home include combustion in gas stoves and heaters and breakdown of cooking oils.

Formaldehyde is emitted from urea-formaldehyde foam insulation. It is also released from particleboard and plywood in which urea-formaldehyde is used as a bonding agent. The rate of release varies with temperature, humidity, light exposure, quality and age of components, formulation, and expertise of the installer (Hollowell et al., 1979a; Rumack, 1978). Andersen et al. (1975) developed a mathematical model that reproduced the measurements of airborne formaldehyde in dwellings and in a climate chamber containing chipboard, with correlation coefficients of 0.88 and 0.94, respectively. There are no studies that document the contribution of permanent-press fabrics and other textiles to formaldehyde concentrations in domestic environments.

Hollowell et al. (1979a) measured total aliphatic aldehyde in indoor air. After human occupation of an experimental house, total aldehydes increased threefold to 0.116 ppm. The ventilation rate was 0.2 air exchanges each hour. A recent study of 15 occupied residential units revealed formaldehyde concentrations of less than 0.12 ppm in 11 of the units (USCPSC, 1979). Concentrations as high as 0.38 and 0.31 ppm were found in two of the units, which were mobile homes containing particleboard.

Formaldehyde concentrations of 0.03-2.5 ppm were measured in 74 mobile homes whose occupants complained of odor and irritation thought to be associated with the use of particle board (Breysse, 1977). Approximately two-thirds of the measurements showed concentrations of less than 0.5 ppm and 90% below 1 ppm. Symptoms experienced by the occupants included drowsiness, nausea, headache, and irritation of eyes, nose, and respiratory tract. Repeat measurements on two homes indicated half-lives (time for concentrations to decrease by 50%) of 45 and 110 d. A Scandinavian study using field tests and mathematical models indicated a half-life of 2 yr (Hollowell et al., 1979b). The ventilation rate was 0.3 air changes each hour. The half-lives depend heavily on air temperature, ventilation rate, surface area of the various products, type of material, and volume of the residence.

The original Breysse (1977) study was extended from 74 to 278 mobile homes and 325 person who experienced symptoms (Tabershaw et al., 1979). Data on the airborne formaldehyde concentrations were not available. Approximately 30% reported eye irritation, 33% irritation of the respiratory tract, and 2% nasal irritation. Headaches and drowsiness were present in 19% and 10%, respectively.

Since 1978, the U.S. Consumer Product Safety Commission (1978) has received more than 500 complaints from consumers whose homes had urea-formaldehyde foam insulation. In-depth investigations of only 100 cases have been completed. Tabulations of complaints indicated that most symptoms were associated with upper airway and eye irritation. Airborne formaldehyde concentrations ranged from 0.01 to 31.7 ppm.

The Connecticut State Department of Health investigated 80 complaints from consumers who had installed urea-formaldehyde foam insulation in their homes (Sardinas et al., 1979). The insulation had been installed 3 wk-1.5 yr before the survey. With formaldehyde at 0.5-10 ppm, 69% of the occupants reported eye irritation, 51% upper respiratory tract complaints, 44% gastrointestinal tract symptoms, 59% headaches, and 40% skin problems. In homes with formaldehyde at less than 0.5 ppm, 31% complained of eye irritation, 49% upper respiratory symptoms, 41% headaches, and 60% skin problems. More than 50% of the individuals questioned reported symptoms when formaldehyde was not detectable using Drager Tubes (minimum detection limit, 0.5 ppm).

The Wisconsin Division of Health (1978) investigated 47 complaints involving 85 consumers. Air sampling for formaldehyde in 20 homes, including 17 mobile homes, revealed a range of 0.02-4.15 ppm and a median of 0.51 ppm. A review of symptoms in 62 of the consumers indicated that 73% had eye irritation, 53% upper respiratory tract irritation, 24% respiratory difficulty, 23% headache and tiredness, 13% nausea, and 14% a history of allergies. Hospitalizations were reported for 2 adults, and for 6 infants with exposures at 0.67-4.82 ppm. The study included 11 pregnant women. Low birth weight and apnea were reported in 3 infants delivered among this exposed group. Detailed investigations of the infants and pregnant women were not available.

SHORT-TERM STUDIES

Metabolism

Formaldehyde is a normal metabolite in mammalian systems and, in small quantities, is rapidly metabolized (Akabane, 1970). The major route of biotransformation appears to be oxidation to formic acid followed by further oxidation to carbon dioxide and water (Buss et al., 1964; Williams, 1959). Administration of radiolabeled formaldehyde to rats by the oral or intraperitoneal route resulted in 40% and 82%, respectively, of the label being found in respiratory carbon dioxide (Neely, 1964; Williams, 1959). The remaining isotope in the intraperitoneal study was in urine as methionine, serine, and an adduct formed from cysteine and formaldehyde (Neely, 1964).

Numerous enzymes capable of catalyzing the reaction of formaldehyde to formic acid have been identified in liver preparations and erythrocytes (Tephly et al. 1974; Utolia and Koivusalo, 1974). Williams (1959) characterized formaldehyde as a compound that reacts rapidly with amino acids, histones, and proteins to form both reversible methylol adducts and stable methylene bridges.

Mortality

Reported LD_{50} values of formaldehyde for the rat after oral administration ranged from 550 to 800 mg/kg (Tsuchiya et al., 1975; Smyth et al., 1941). The LC_{50} values for rats at 0.5 and 4 h were 820 and 482 ppm, respectively (Skog, 1950; Nagornyi et al., 1979). Pulmonary edema was the predominant pathologic change at these concentrations. Similar results were obtained in mice and cats (Nagornyi et al., 1979; Iwanoff, 1911).

Effects on the Eye

Formaldehyde is a severe eye irritant. Application of a drop of formalin to rabbit eyes caused edema of the cornea and conjunctiva and iritis, graded 8 on a scale of 1-10 (Carpenter and Smyth, 1946). Exposure of rabbits and guinea pigs to airborne formaldehyde at 40-70 ppm for 10 d produced some lacrimation, but no corneal injury (Grant, 1974).

Potts et al. (1955) injected formaldehyde intravenously (0.9 g/kg) in monkeys over several hours and observed an immediate change in the electroretinogram, but no blindness.

Effects on the Skin

Formaldehyde can cause skin irritation and is a potent allergen. Mild to moderate irritation developed when formaldehyde was applied to guinea pig skin in concentrations of 0.1-20% (Colburn, 1970). Guinea pigs are readily sensitized with intradermal injections (Draize method), topical occluded applications (Buehler method) and open epicutaneous tests (OET method) (Klecak, 1977; Magnusson and Kligman, 1977; Marzulli and Maibach, 1977). With open applications, a 3% solution of formaldehyde sensitized guinea pigs, whereas a 1% solution did not (Maibach, 1978). Preexisting sensitivity was elicited with concentrations down to 3% by open challenge, and 1% or less by closed-patch challenge. In another study, nine guinea pigs were administered formaldehyde intradermally or topically at 0.1-1% over a 2-wk period (Colburn, 1970). After a 2-wk rest period, the animals were challenged with formaldehyde at 0.01-5% and 2 d later at 0.02%; five became sensitized.

Effects on the Respiratory Tract

Formaldehyde is extremely soluble in mucous membranes of the respiratory tract. Egle (1972) concluded that retention is nearly 100% in dogs, regardless of ventilation rate, tidal volume, region of the respiratory tract exposed, or formaldehyde concentration.

Exposure for 10 min to 3.1 ppm produced a 50% decrease in respiratory rate (RD_{50}) of mice (Kane and Alarie, 1977). Utilizing a tracheal cannula to deliver formaldehyde, these authors showed that the upper respiratory tract was the site of reactions that provoked the decrease in respiratory rate. Repeated exposures at 1.0 and 3.1 ppm, 3 h/d for 4 d revealed that the maximum percent decrease in respiratory rate was reached after about 4-8 min, and increased each day. After the plateau was reached, there was a reduction in the percentage decrease during the rest of the exposure. There was complete recovery between the daily exposures.

Concentrations of formaldehyde at 0.3-50 ppm significantly increased airway resistance and decreased lung compliance in guinea pigs after 1 h of exposure (Amdur, 1960). The magnitude of the effects were dose-dependent over the range of concentrations tested. These effects were reversible within 1 h after exposure at concentrations of 0.3-11 ppm. No effect was observed in guinea pigs exposed at 0.05 ppm for 1 h. Tracheal cannulation resulted in a greater increase in airway resistance, and the combination of formaldehyde and submicron particle size sodium chloride aerosol at 3-30 mg/m^3 increased resistance even further. Other research has shown formaldehyde to depress ciliary activity within 10 min when tracheal preparations were exposed at concentrations of 20-100 ppm (Cralley, 1942; Dalhamn and Rosengren, 1971).

Effects on the Nervous System

Kulle and Cooper (1975) reported that a 1 h exposure to formaldehyde at 0.5-2.5 ppm decreased rat nasopalatine nerve response to amyl alcohol. A partial recovery of the neural response occurred when the nasal cavities were perfused with air for 1 h after the formaldehyde exposure. Bonashevskaya (1973) exposed rats at 0.83 and 2.5 ppm for 3 mo. Histologic and histochemical changes were observed in the neurons and dendrite receptor synaptic apparatus in the cerebral amygdaloid complex. No histologic changes were observed in the central nervous system of monkeys injected with formaldehyde intravenously (0.9 g/kg) over several hours (Potts et al., 1955).

PROLONGED STUDIES

A 90-d study was conducted with formaldehyde administered in the drinking water of rats on a weight/volume basis at 50, 100, and 150 mg/kg body weight/d (Monsanto, 1973a) or mixed in the diet so that dogs received 50, 75, and 100 mg/kg body weight/d (Monsanto, 1973b). There were no significant effects on hematologic (hematocrit, hemoglobin, and total and differential leukocyte counts) and biochemical (blood sugar, blood urea nitrogen, alkaline phosphatase, and serum glutamic oxaloacetic transaminase) parameters, or in several organs examined histologically. The highest dose administered to each species produced a decrease in weight gain.

Groups of 25 male rats were continuously exposed to formaldehyde by inhalation at 1.6, 4.6, or 8 ppm for up to 3 mo (Dubreuil et al., 1976). The only effect observed at the low dose was a yellowing of fur. The intermediate-dose group also showed decreased body weight. The group exposed at 8 ppm for 60 d showed eye and upper respiratory irritation, decreased body weight gain, and decreased liver weight. In another inhalation study, rats, guinea pigs, rabbits, monkeys, and dogs were exposed continuously at 3.8 ppm for 90 d (Coon et al., 1970). One of 15 exposed rats died, but no other signs of toxicity were observed. Various degrees of interstitial inflammation were seen in the lungs of all exposed animals. Focal chronic inflammation was also observed in the hearts and kidneys of the rats and guinea pigs. The authors were uncertain whether these inflammatory changes resulted from exposure to formaldehyde.

Groups of 60 mice were exposed to airborne formaldehyde at 41.5, 83, or 166 ppm 1 h/d, three times a week for up to 35 wk (Horton et al., 1963). Pathologic examination of the tracheal epithelium revealed basal cell hyperplasia, squamous cell metaplasia, and atypical metaplasia. Metaplasia extended into the major bronchi in the 41.5-ppm group after exposure at 125 ppm for an additional 29 wk. Exposure of mice at 166 ppm was terminated after 11 d, owing to intoxication and high death rate. In a noncontinuous inhalation study, mice and rats were exposed at 4, 12.7, and 39 ppm, 6 h/d, 5 d/wk (Battelle Columbus Laboratories, 1977a). No adverse effects were observed in the 4 ppm group exposed for 13 weeks. At 12.7 ppm for 13 weeks, decrease in body weight was observed; 2 of the 20 exposed rats showed evidence of nasal erosion. The 39-ppm exposure was terminated after 2 wk because of severe changes in nasal mucosa, including ulceration and necrosis.

In another study, 25 rats each were exposed continuously for 3 mo at 0.0098, 0.028, 0.82, and 2.4 ppm (Fel'dman and Bonashevskaya, 1971). The authors reported that at 2.4 ppm there was a significant decrease in cholinesterase activity, and at 0.82 and 2.4 ppm proliferation of lymphocytes and histiocytes in the lungs and some peribronchial and perivascular hyperemia. Exposure at the two lowest concentrations resulted in no significant findings.

CARCINOGENIC POTENTIAL

Mice exposed to formaldehyde at 83 ppm, for 1 h, 3 d/wk for 35 wk or at 41.5 ppm for 1 h, 3 d/wk for 35 wk and at 125 ppm for an additional 29 wk showed basal cell hyperplasia and squamous cell metaplasia in the tracheobronchial epithelium but no tumors (Horton et al., 1963). Hamsters exposed at 10 ppm for 5 h, 5 d/wk for their lifetime (average, 18 mo) showed increased cell proliferation and hyperplasia in the lungs (Nettsheim, 1976). This investigator also reported that weekly 5-h exposures at 50 ppm for lifetime (18 mo) produced squamous metaplasia, but no tumors.

Fischer 344 rats and B6C3F1 mice (120/sex/concentration) are being exposed to formaldehyde at 0, 2, 6, and 15 ppm for 6 h/d, 5 d/wk in a Chemical Industry Institute of Toxicology (CIIT) sponsored study at Battelle Columbus Laboratories (CIIT, 1979b). Preliminary results indicated that 15 ppm caused multifocal squamous cell metaplasia of nasal epithelium in 6 of 20 rats at both the 6- and the 12-mo sacrifice. Histologic examinations of 3 additional rats with enlarged noses after 15, 15, and 16 mo of exposure demonstrated squamous cell carcinomas in the nasomaxillary epithelium. A single squamous cell carcinoma of the skin was seen after 10 mo in the group of rats exposed at 6 ppm; this tumor was not of the same type observed at 15 ppm and did not invade the nasal epithelium. Additional preliminary results have shown the presence of nasal carcinomas in 8 of 40 rats exposed at 15 ppm and sacrificed at 18 mo and nasal carcinomas in 29 other rats exposed at 15 ppm that were moribund or died spontaneously between the sixteenth and eighteenth months (CIIT, 1980). Additional tumors have not been found in the group exposed at 6 ppm. A small adenomatous polyp was found in one of 40 rats exposed at 2 ppm and sacrificed at 18 mo. Epithelial dysplasia and squamous metaplasia of the turbinates were observed in rats in all three exposure groups, the magnitude of the effects being dose-related. No control rats or any mice have shown histopathologic changes or tumor development of the kinds found in exposed rats. This is the first study to implicate formaldehyde as a potential experimental carcinogen, but the significance of these preliminary findings can be evaluated only after completion of the study and analysis of the pathologic findings.

Injection-site sarcomas developed in 2 of 10 rats given weekly injections of 0.4% aqueous formaldehyde for 15 mo (Watanabe et al., 1954). Fibrosarcomas were observed in the liver and omentum in 2 other rats. These results are not meaningful, because of lack of controls and inappropriateness of the route of administration.

Rusch et al. ([1980]) exposed rats to HCl at a mean concentration of 10.7 ppm and formaldehyde at 10.3 ppm for 6 h/d, 5 d/wk for 410 exposures over 618 d. Before dilution to the stated concentrations in the exposure chamber, the initial reaction mixture had average HCl and formaldehyde concentrations of 6,567 and 1,021 ppm, respectively; alkylating-agent activity of 1,813 ppb was also detected, possibly as a result of the interaction of HCl and formaldehyde in the gas phase. Alkylating-agent activity in the animal exposure chamber, as measured by chromatography, was 28 ppb. Preliminary results of histologic examinations on 56 exposed animals indicated a 14% incidence of squamous cell carcinoma of the nasal epithelium after 589 d. Tumors of this kind were not observed in controls. One of the alkylating agents identified in the chamber was bis(chloromethyl) ether (BCME), at a concentration of approximately 0.1 ppb. BCME is a potent carcinogen; esthesioneuroepitheliomas of the nose, squamous cell carcinomas of the lung and nasal turbinates, and adenocarcinomas of the lung and nasal cavity were produced in rats after exposure to BCME at 0.1 ppm 6 h/d, 5 d/wk for 10-100 exposures (Kuschner et al., 1975).

The carcinogenic potential of hexamethylenetetramine (HMT), which can decompose in an acid media to release formaldehyde and ammonia, has been examined (Della Porta et al., 1968). Mice and rats were given fresh solutions of HMT in drinking water every 24 h at 0.5-5% for 30-60 wk and at 1-5% for 2-104 wk, respectively. Mice were observed for up to 130 wk and rats for up to 3 yr. At 5% HMT, there was 50% mortality in the rats after 2 wk. No significant effects on growth or survival were observed in any of the other groups of rats or the mice. Histologic examination indicated that no effects were attributable to HMT. No carcinogenic activity was observed.

MUTAGENIC POTENTIAL

Numerous studies have been conducted to determine the mutagenicity of formaldehyde, and Auerbach et al. (1977) have reviewed the subject extensively. Formaldehyde has exhibited mutagenic activity in a wide variety of organisms, but the mechanism of formaldehyde mutagenesis has not been resolved. Formaldehyde may cause mutations by reacting directly with DNA; by forming mutagenic products on reaction with amino groups on simple amines, amino acids, nucleic acids, or proteins; or by oxidizing to peroxides that can react directly with DNA or indirectly by free-radical formation.

Mutagenic activity has been reported in E. coli (Bilimoria, 1975) and Pseudomonas fluorescens (Englesberg, 1952), but not in the Ames strains of Salmonella typhimurium (Koops and Butterworth, 1976). Weak mutagenic activity was observed when the fungi Neurospora crassa and Aspergillus nidulans were treated (Auerbach et al., 1977). The increase in mutagenic activity observed in these studies after treatment in the presence of catalase inhibitors suggested that peroxides were involved in the induction of mutations. Formaldehyde induced mitotic recombination in Saccharomyces cerevisiae (Chanet et al., 1975). The studies concerning formaldehyde mutagenesis in Drosophila have been reviewed by several authors (Auerbach et al., 1977; Rapoport, 1948; Solyanik et al., 1972). Mutations were induced in male larvae fed formaldehyde-containing food and in adults injected with aqueous solutions of formaldheyde. The exposure of adults or larvae to formaldehyde vapors has not produced mutations. In one of five species of grasshoppers, formaldehyde caused chromosomal damage (Manna and Parida, 1967). Germinating barley seeds soaked in formaldehyde solutions did not give evidence of mutation on maturation (Ehrenberg et al., 1956).

The mutagenic potential of formaldehyde in mammalian systems has not been thoroughly studied. An increase in mutation frequency was observed when formaldehyde was tested in the L5178Y mouse lymphoma assay (Gosser and Butterworth, 1977), according to the published procedure (Clive and Spector, 1975). A clear dose-response relationship was evident in only one of four experiments. No mutagenic activity was observed when formaldehyde was tested in the Chinese hamster ovary cell/HGPRT assay (Hsie et al., 1978). Likewise, no effect was observed in dominant lethal studies conducted with Swiss mice (Epstein et al., 1972).

Although formaldehyde exhibits mutagenic activity in a variety of microorganisms and in some insects, more work is necessary to ascertain the potential of this compound to cause mutations in germinal or somatic mammalian cells.

EMBRYOTOXIC/TERATOGENIC POTENTIAL

There were no adverse gonadotropic or reproductive effects in male rats administered formaldehyde at 0.1 ppm in drinking water or 0.4 ppm in the air for 6 mo (Guseva, 1972). Pregnant dogs fed diets containing 125 or 375 ppm on days 4-56 of pregnancy showed no evidence of teratogenesis (Hurni and Ohder, 1973). There was no effect on the course of pregnancy and no malformations in the offspring when rats were exposed at 4 ppm, 4 h/d during days 1-19 of pregnancy (Sheveleva, 1971).

Gofmekler (1968) exposed female rats to airborne formaldehyde at 0.8 and 0.01 ppm for 10-15 d before placing them with males. All animals were then exposed for 6-10 d at the same concentrations of formaldehyde. Day of mating was not recorded and duration of gestational exposure was unknown. No gross abnormalities were observed in the offspring, but there was a 14-15% increase in duration of pregnancy, compared with controls. Although the surviving offspring of exposed mothers averaged slightly greater body weights than the offspring of controls, the lungs and livers of offspring of exposed mothers were smaller than those of controls. Histologically, the livers of the offspring of mothers exposed at 0.01 ppm were not different from those of controls. In the group from mothers exposed at 0.8 ppm, the livers showed increased extramedullary hematopoietic centers and epithelial proliferation in the common bile duct. Additional studies are needed before firm conclusions can be made about the teratogenic potential of airborne formaldehyde at low concentrations.

Dogs fed HMT at 600 and 1,250 ppm on days 4-56 of pregnancy did not show evidence of teratogenesis (Hurni and Ohder, 1973). Likewise, long-term feeding studies of rats given 0.16% HMT showed no effect on the reproductive capacity of rats (Natvig et al., 1971).

EFFECTS ON HUMANS

CONTROLLED EXPERIMENTS WITH AIRBORNE FORMALDEHYDE

Several controlled-exposure studies have provided valuable dose-response data on the irritant effects of airborne formaldehyde. The information from these studies on the percentages of the exposed populations responding at various formaldehyde concentrations is summarized in Tables 4 and 5.

Sixteen healthy young subjects were exposed to formaldehyde at 0.25 0.42, 0.83, or 1.6 ppm 5 h/d for 4 d (Andersen, 1979). Measures of physiologic parameters, subjective discomfort, and mathematical performance were made in the control period and after 1-3 and 3-5 h of exposure. No significant changes were observed in pulmonary function, nor was there any difference in performance of mathematical tests between the control period and exposure to formaldehyde. The nasal-mucus flow rate was decreased at all concentrations except 0.83 ppm; the effect was observed only in the upper third of the nose. When asked about their subjective response to formaldehyde, subjects exposed at the four increasing formaldehyde concentrations reported "slight discomfort" averaging 9, 5, 11, and 18, respectively, on a scale of zero to 100. Specifically, the subjects complained of conjunctival irritation and dryness of the nose and throat.

In a second study, 33 subjects (24 men and 9 women) were exposed to formaldehyde at 0.03-3.2 ppm for a total of 35 min, and 48 others (35 men and 13 women) were exposed at 0.03-4 ppm for 1.5 min (Weber-Tschopp et al., 1977). Several responses were measured, such as eye, nose, and throat irritation, odor, "desire to leave the room," and eye-blinking rate. An approximately linear relationship was found for the average responses over the range of concentrations. At 0.03 ppm, there was no difference in the average response between exposure to formaldehyde and control air. Significant changes began to appear at 1.2 ppm. The thresholds for the specific responses (shown in Table 5) ranged from 1.2 to 2.1 ppm. There was some suggestion of adaptation to the irritating effects of formaldehyde: at the same concentrations, responses to 1.5-min exposures were generally greater than the responses during 35-min exposures.

The eye-irritation response to exposures to formaldehyde for 5 min at 0.01 to 1.0 ppm was investigated in 12 subjects (Schuck et al., 1966). Subjective eye irritation was scored on a scale of zero to 24. Between 0.3 and 1.0 ppm, there was a linear increase in the average reported eye-irritation response, ranging from light irritation (just noticeable) to severe irritation. At concentrations below 0.3 ppm, a linear relationship was not found. Subjects experienced similar light irritation and eye-blinking rates at 0.05 ppm as they did at 0.5 ppm. The range of sensitivity to formaldehyde was evident by comparing the effects in two subjects. At 0.8 ppm, one reported barely noticeable irritation, while a second had severe irritation, including lacrimation. A complicating factor in this study was that, because of the method for generating formaldehyde, peroxyacetyl nitrate, nitrogen dioxide, and ethylene were present in the chamber.

PHYSIOLOGIC ENDPOINTS

Acute ingestion of formalin by humans has resulted in loss of consciousness, vascular collapse, pneumonia, hemorrhagic nephritis, and abortion. Formaldehyde has occasionally injured the larnyx and trachea, but damage to the gastrointestinal tract occurred primarily in the stomach and lower esophagus. Fatalities have resulted from ingestion of as little as 30 ml of formalin (Bohmer, 1934; Kline, 1925). The use of formaldehyde to devitalize dental pulp has produced paresthesia, soft-tissue necrosis, and sequestration of bone (Grossman, 1978; Heling et al., 1977; Montgomery, 1976). Filters impregnated with melamine-formaldehyde resin were associated with an outbreak of hemolytic anemia among hemodialysis patients (Orringer and Mattern, 1976).

Skin

Contact of the skin with formaldehyde may cause primary irritation or allergic dermatitis (Glass, 1961; Pirila and Kilpio, 1949). Rostenberg et al. (1952) reported eczematous sensitivity to formalin in nurses who handled thermometers that had been immersed in a 10% solution of formaldehyde. A similar outbreak occurred in a hemodialysis unit where a 2% formalin solution was used to sterilize open tanks (Blejer and Miller, 1966). Dermatitis has been reported after contact with nail-hardeners, textiles, resins, and gaseous formaldehyde (Engle and Calnan, 1966; Fisher et al., 1962; Lazar, 1966; Logan and Perry, 1973; O'Quinn and Kennedy, 1965). Allergy to formaldehyde resins may be the result of unreacted formaldehyde or formaldehyde arising from decomposition, other resin ingredients, or the resin itself (USDHEW, 1976a). The human data must be divided between two eras: earlier studies when 5% formaldehyde (in water) was the standard diagnostic concentration; and recent studies with 2% (in water) (Epstein and Maibach, 1966). The 5% formaldehyde concentration was unusually high for diagnostic purposes; even the 2% concentration is near the generally-accepted irritancy threshold, so these results also provide a sensitization rate much greater than would be expected for the general population. (North American Contact Dermatitis Group, 1973).

Formaldehyde has been shown to be a potent experimental allergen in humans. Skin sensitization was produced in about 8% of male subjects given repeated occlusive applications of 5 or 10% aqueous formaldehyde for 3.5 wk and then challenged with a 1% application 2 wk later (Marzulli and Maibach, 1973). Approximately 4% of 1,200 dermatology patients exhibited positive skin reactions when tested with 2% formalin (0.8% formaldehyde) under an occlusive patch (Rudner et al., 1973). Experiments suggest that most sensitized subjects can tolerate exposure to aqueous formaldehyde at 30 ppm (0.003%), applied to the axilla (Jordan et al., 1979; Maibach and Franz, [1980]). Sensitized subjects who tolerate formaldehyde-containing products may react to occluded-patch tests at lower concentrations; Marzulli and Maibach (1973) reported that 1/5 sensitized subjects reacted at a challenge concentration as low as 0.01%.

Although formaldehyde is a potent experimental allergen in man and animals, many of the daily exposures to formaldehyde (in shampoos, clothing, etc.) may involve quantities below the threshold for sensitization induction and elicitation or contact times less than that required to produce a response (Marzulli and Maibach, 1977). More complete quantitative induction and elicitation studies combined with provocative use tests should allow more realistic risk assessments.

Contact urticaria also occurs with formaldehyde (Odom and Maibach, 1977); however, epidemiologic data are not available, nor has the mechanism (type A, B or C) been identified.

Eyes

Formaldehyde acts as a mucous-membrane irritant to cause conjunctivitis and lacrimation. Eye irritation is a common complaint and has been reported at airborne concentrations of 0.3-0.9 ppm in industrial workers (Bourne and Seferian, 1959; Morrill, 1961). Severe eye irritation can develop in the range of 4-20 ppm (Barnes and Speicher, 1942; Walker, 1964). Controlled human exposures indicated that the group threshold for eye irritation was 1.2 ppm, and for eye-blinking rate was 1.7 ppm (Weber-Tschopp et al., 1977). The eye blinking rate was doubled in 33% of the subjects exposed at 2.1 ppm and in 11% of those exposed at 0.5 ppm. A linear relationship was found for eye irritation in exposed subjects, from a group response of no irritation at 0.03 ppm to some irritation at 3.2 ppm. Tolerance to eye irritation was reported after exposure at 13.8 ppm for 10 min (Sim and Pattle, 1957). A complete visual-test battery and ophthalmologic examination of workers exposed at 1.5 ppm revealed no effects of formaldehyde on the eyes (USDHEW, 1976b). However, Schuck et al. (1966) found a linear relationship between eye irritation and formaldehyde concentration over a range of 0.3-1 ppm; these responses ranged from light to severe irritation. The authors determined that formaldehyde and peroxyacetyl nitrate accounted for 80% and 20%, respectively, of the eye irritation associated with photochemical air pollution.

Respiratory System

Formaldehyde has been reported to cause irritation and dryness of the nose and throat and olfactory fatigue. Upper airway irritation attributed to formaldehyde at 1-11 ppm occurred in employees handling nylon fabric coated with urea-formaldehyde resin (Ettinger and Jeremias, 1955). Customers in dress shops have complained of burning and stinging of the eyes, headaches, and nose and throat irritation with formaldehyde at 0.13-0.45 ppm (Bourne and Seferian, 1959). Similar complaints, along with disturbed sleep and unusual thirst, were reported by workers at a paper-conditioning installation (Morrill, 1961). Airborne formaldehyde concentrations released from paper treated with urea-formaldehyde or melamine-formaldehyde resin were found to be 0.9-1.6 ppm. Annoying odor, constant prickling irritation of mucous membranes, wheezing, tearing, excessive thirst, and disturbed sleep were reported by employees in eight textile plants (Shipkovitz, 1968). The prevalence of respiratory illness and complaints was more than 15% in four plants and 5-15% in the other four. Airborne formaldehyde was measured at 0-2.7 ppm, with an average of 0.68 ppm. Workers in a garment factory were examined by the California Department of Public Health; airborne concentrations ranged from 0.9-2.7 ppm (Blejer and Miller, 1966). Employees reported increased eye and upper respiratory tract irritation in areas where large quantities of partially completed permanent-press fabrics accumulated. Olfactory adaptation to the irritant effects of formaldehyde occurred within 30 min of exposure, but after a 1- to 2-h interruption of exposure irritation returned (Blejer and Miller, 1966; Kerfoot and Mooney, 1975; Shipkovitz, 1968).

Kerfoot and Mooney (1975) surveyed six funeral homes that used formaldehyde and paraformaldehyde in the embalming process. The average airborne concentrations in the embalming rooms were 0.25-1.39 ppm. The investigations noted eye and upper respiratory tract irritation in some employees.

A cross-sectional study of rubber workers exposed to a hexamethylene-tetramine-resorcinol resin revealed significant decreases in small airway function over the course of the workshift and an excess of symptoms such as chest tightness, eye and nose irritation, and cough (Gamble et al., 1976). No difference was found in baseline lung function tests between exposed and control groups. Chemical analysis of respirable particles was not performed and no association was found between airborne levels of resorcinol, formaldehyde, hydrogen cyanide, or ammonia and changes in pulmonary function. A study of employees producing filters with phenol-formaldehyde impregnated fibers indicated that pulmonary function ($FEV_{1.0}$/FVC and MEF50%/FVC) measured at the beginning of the Monday shift was significantly lower in employees who had worked more than 5 yr compared to those never involved in production (Shoenberg and Mitchell, 1975). Chronic symptoms—chronic cough and excess phlegm—were increased in the group currently involved in production. Acute symptoms included eye, nose, and throat irritation and cough; however, little change was observed in the employees' FVC, $FEV_{1.0}$, and MEF50% during the course of a workweek or workday. Formaldehyde was not systematically measured, but two surveys reported concentrations of 0.4-0.8 ppm and 9.14 ppm. The latter was thought to be atypical of the usual exposure conditions in the plant. Other pulmonary irritants present in the work environment included phenol and acrylic-fiber breakdown products.

Lower airway irritation may be evidenced by cough, chest tightness, and wheezing. One man developed dyspnea and asthma after acute inhalation of formalin vapor (Zannini and Russo, 1957). Clinical examination revealed pulmonary edema with a 40% decrease in vital capacity. A neurology resident developed actue respiratory distress after 15 h of exposure to formaldehyde (Porter, 1975). Auscultation of the chest revealed diffuse rales and occasional rhonchi. Chest x-ray revealed early pulmonary edema. The resident was known to have marked atopy to a wide range of allergens. Pulmonary edema, pneumonitis, and death may occur after inhalation of formaldehyde at concentrations exceeding 50 ppm (Fassett, 1963).

Nervous System

Olfactory fatigue with increased olfactory thresholds to rosemary, thymol, camphor, and tar were observed among plywood and particleboard workers (Weger, 1927; Yefremov, 1970). Numerous nonspecific symptoms related to nervous system response have been mentioned. Formaldehyde from resins used in construction produced thirst, headaches, dizziness, apathy, and inability to concentrate (Helwig, 1977). Workers exposed to phenol-formaldehyde resins complained of headaches, dizziness, disturbed sleep, weakness, and apathy (Weger, 1927). Studies in the USSR showed no electroencephalographic (EEG) changes in five subjects exposed to formaldehyde at 0.03 ppm, but these subjects did respond with EEG changes at 0.044 ppm (Fel'dman and Bonashevskaya, 1971).

SUMMARY OF ANIMAL AND HUMAN EXPOSURE TO FORMALDEHYDE

ANIMAL EXPOSURE

Formaldehyde is irritating to the eyes and upper respiratory tract of laboratory animals. When given orally, it is moderately toxic and causes severe erosion of gastrointestinal tissue. It is a known skin irritant and, through repeated contact with dilute solutions, can produce allergic sensitization.

Concentrations of 0.3-50 ppm increased airway resistance and decreased lung compliance after 1 h of exposure. Exposure of mice at 1 and 3 ppm produced a decrease in respiratory rate. Interim results of a chronic inhalation study have shown squamous cell carcinomas in the nasomaxillary epithelium of rats exposed at 15 ppm, 6 h/d, 5 d/wk for 18 mo. There is no published evidence that formaldehyde is carcinogenic in animals.

Formaldehyde, either itself or as HMT, does not appear to interfere with reproduction, nor is there evidence of malformations in offspring of exposed parents. It has been shown to be mutagenic in several nonmammalian systems, particularly microorganisms and insects, but standard screens, such as the Ames test and Chinesee hamster ovary cell/HGPRT assay, have shown no evidence of mutagenicity.

Results of animal studies are summarized in Tables 1 and 2.

HUMAN EXPOSURES

People may be exposed to formaldehyde in industry and in the outdoor-ambient and indoor-residential environments. Automotive exhaust, smog, cigarette smoke, incinerators, and decomposition of formaldehyde-derived products are sources of indoor and outdoor exposure. Numerous consumer complaints have been associated with urea-formaldehyde products in the domestic environment. Eye and upper respiratory tract irritation, headaches, and gastrointestinal problems are the predominant symptoms associated with exposure to formaldehyde. Skin irritation and allergic dermatitis have also resulted from exposure, and experiments have shown that individuals can become sensitized.

Results of human studies can be found in Tables 3, 4, and 5.

ANALYTICAL METHODS

Knowledge of the sensitivity and accuracy of the analytical method used in measuring a pollutant concentration is important not only in determining whether a concentration can be measured for comparison with a recommended airborne exposure limit, but also in evaluating inhalation studies on a particular compound. Often, methods of analysis are not reported; this makes it difficult to judge whether reported airborne concentrations are accurate.

The analytical methods for measuring airborne formaldehdye have been extensively reviewed (USDHEW, 1976a; NRC, [1980]) and are briefly summarized here. Spectrophotometric methods are most commonly used for determining the formaldehyde concentrations in indoor environments; chromotropic acid (4,5-dihydroxy-2,7-naphthalenedisulfonic acid) and pararosaniline are the most widely used reagents. The APHA Intersociety Committee (1972) and the National Institute for Occupational Safety and Health (USDHEW, 1976a) have recommended a modified chromotropic acid method for estimation of formaldehyde in air. The sensitivity of this method is 0.1 µg/ml of sample solution, or approximately 0.04 ppm in sampled air. There are some deficiencies with this method, such as interferences from other substances, e.g., nitrogen dioxide, acrolein, and phenol, which can be encountered in indoor air. The Lawrence Berkeley Laboratory has been developing a pararosaniline technique that does not appear to be subject to interferences (Miksch et al., [1980]). The estimated minimal detection concentration is 0.06 ppm. Methods using other reagents are also available, but either they have not been adequately tested or they have major drawbacks, such as instability or interference from other chemicals. Table 6 summarizes the spectrophotometric methods for formaldehyde.

Microwave, infrared, and laser fluorescence spectroscopy have been studied as alternatives to spectrophotometry (NRC, [1980]). However, these require sophisticated maintenance and support facilities and are seldom portable. Chromatographic methods have not gained acceptance, because of problems with interference and lack of sensitivity. A method for detecting formaldehyde by measuring the chemiluminescence resulting from the alkaline peroxide oxidation of formaldehyde and gallic acid has been reported to detect concentrations as low as 3.0 ng/ml. One drawback of this method is that it is not specific for formaldehyde.

INHALATION EXPOSURE LIMITS

Recommended and promulgated formaldehyde exposure limits issued by various countries are listed in Table 7. The present Occupational Safety and Health Administration (OSHA, 1979) federal workplace standard for formaldehyde is 3 ppm, as a time-weighted average concentration over an 8-h workshift. The American Conference of Governmental Industrial Hygienists (ACGIH, 1974) recommends a threshold limit value-ceiling (TLV-C) for formaldehyde of 2 ppm, because of "generalized complaints of irritation from formaldehyde at levels well below 5 ppm." ACGIH originally recommended a TLV-C of 5 ppm, but reduced the concentration to 2 ppm in 1972 (ACGIH, 1972). A TLV of 5 ppm was believed "low enough to prevent respiratory injury ... but does not provide freedom from irritation of all exposed individuals" (ACGIH, 1974). The National Institute for Occupational Safety and Health (USDHEW, 1976a) recommends a workplace ceiling limit for formaldehyde of 1 ppm, because of reports of irritation, objectionable odor, and disturbed sleep after exposure at 0.3 ppm and generalized complaints at concentrations above 1 ppm. It also states that individuals sensitized to formaldehyde should not be further exposed.

The Environmental Protection Agency has not promulgated an ambient-air quality standard for formaldehyde in the United States. Kane et al. (1979) have suggested that an animal model be used to establish concentration ranges for exposure standards. On the basis of the RD_{50} in mice of 3.1 ppm and using a factor of 10^{-3} to protect the entire population, these authors arrived at 0.003 ppm as a no-effect level appropriate for an air-quality standard. Experimental evidence and commonly available analytical techniques do not exist to support such a standard. The suggested concentration is below the limits of detectability for most analytical methods for formaldehyde and lower than background concentrations of formaldehyde. The American Industrial Hygiene Association (1968) recommended a community air-quality standard for formaldehyde of 0.1 ppm; a concentration they believed would prevent sensory irritation in an exposed population. The West Germans have promulgated an outdoor ambient-air standard for formaldehyde of 0.025 ppm (Andersen et al, 1975).

Several foreign countries currently are establishing indoor-air formaldehyde standards. In 1978, the Netherlands promulgated a standard of 0.1 ppm (Hollowell et al, 1979b). Sweden, Denmark, and West Germany are considering similar concentrations as indoor standards (Hollowell et al, 1979b). The Danish scientist (Andersen, 1979) who recommended an indoor-air standard stated that the "basis for the setting of any standard for continuous exposure should be that all but the sensitized subjects are protected against adverse health effects." Further, the majority of the subjects should not experience discomfort or decrease of performance.

It should be noted that the preliminary results of an ongoing study (CIIT, 1979b), which is showing squamous cell carcinomas in the nasomaxillary epithelium of rats, were not available when the above-mentioned foreign standards were established; the impact of these new findings on recent recommendations in those countries is not known.

COMMITTEE SUMMARY AND RECOMMENDATIONS

SUMMARY

The health effects associated with exposure to formaldehyde cover a wide range of signs and symptoms. Most are related to the irritating properties of formaldehyde involving the eyes, nose, and throat. The severity of response is related to exposure concentration and can vary from person to person. Responses may be categorized as follows: (1) those which produce discomfort (irritation); (2) those which result in more significant effects, such as increased airway resistance and severe tissue damage in the respiratory tract; and (3) those which result in sensitization. The degree of hypersensitivity to these responses in the population has not been defined.

Two kinds of studies were available for evaluating the above-mentioned responses to formaldehyde: human--including controlled, epidemiologic, and complaint-related investigations--and animal. Epidemiologic studies in the workplace generally were limited because they could not isolate effects produced by formaldehyde. Also, reports of indoor residential exposure have not allowed separation of symptoms where there have been a variety of environmental conditions or diseases. Such reports have been based on consumer complaints and have lacked random sampling and appropriate controls. The prevalence of morbidity associated with exposure to formaldehyde in the residence cannot be determined with the existing data. Nevertheless, complaints have been associated with the use of products containing formaldehyde in homes, where measurements have indicated a wide range of concentrations from 0.01 to 31.7 ppm.

Animal studies were limited; they did not provide dose-response data on the irritating effects reported by humans at low airborne concentration. There are no published data to indicate that formaldehyde is carcinogenic in humans or animals. However, an ongoing lifetime inhalation experiment with rats and mice is showing malignant nasal tumors in rats exposed at 15 ppm and dose-related histologic changes in the noses of rats exposed at 2 and 6 ppm. None of these effects has been found in the mice. Although the preliminary data in rats are not yet amenable to inclusion in an analysis of human risk, the CPSC is urged to reanalyze the risk associated with formaldehyde exposure when all the date of the study in question are available for review.

In the Committee's best judgment, the available controlled human studies are currently the most relevant for evaluation of the risks of formaldehyde in indoor air. These studies measured primary irritancy in test populations and provided dose-response data at various airborne concentrations of formaldehyde. The data from these studies are summarized in Tables 4 and 5. Small numbers of young healthy adults were exposed to various concentrations of formaldehyde for short periods. Concentrations of 1.5-3.0 ppm produced in many test subjects (33% in one study and 94% in another) a variety of effects, including moderate irritation of mucous membranes, increase in odor threshold, decrease in nasal-mucus flow, and doubling of the eye-blinking rate. Fewer subjects (10-20%) experienced strong to moderate irritation and a desire to leave the test atmosphere. No changes in airway resistance were observed.

When these test subjects were exposed to formaldehyde vapors at 0.5-1.5 ppm, the following responses were reported: decrease in nasal-mucus flow, irritation of nose and throat, dryness in nose and throat (94% of subjects in one study), moderate eye irritation (2%), doubling of the eye-blinking rate (11%), and desire to leave the test atmosphere (3%). Airway resistance was measured, and no changes were observed.

Some of these subjects were also exposed to formaldehyde at 0.25 ppm. Slight eye irritation and dryness of the nose and throat were experienced by 19% of the subjects, and a decrease in nasal-mucus flow was experienced by a few.

The responses described in the foregoing were obtained from limited test populations. When such data are applied to the general population, several factors may influence the extent of response, including variability of health status, genetic predisposition to the effects of irritants, and such physiologic characteristics as age, sex, and pregnancy. Any of these factors may cause some individuals to react with greater frequency and severity to concentrations of formaldehyde that produce milder effects in less susceptible individuals.

In addition, responses reported in controlled studies may occur at an increased rate in the general population, because of the interactions between formaldehyde and other irritants in the environment. Irritant effects of formaldehyde in humans are accelerated by the presence of cigarette smoke. The likelihood of interactions with other irritants, such as ozone and oxides of nitrogen, should not be discounted, but quantitative estimation of this combined effect is not now possible.

The foregoing factors should be given serious consideration by the CPSC in the selection of an indoor exposure limit for formaldehyde. Some of the factors might decrease susceptibility; most may increase it.

RECOMMENDATIONS

On the basis of consumer complaints and controlled human studies, irritation appears to be the most sensitive response to formaldehyde. The Committee's best judgment as to a range of irritation responses associated with exposure to various concentrations of formaldehyde is summarized in Table 8. This tabulation was developed from the limited number of controlled human studies, which provide the only dose-response data from human exposure to low airborne concentrations of formaldehyde. Although the extent of irritancy has not been investigated in controlled human studies at concentrations below 0.25 ppm, the Committee expects that less than 20% of an exposed human population would react to such formaldehyde exposure with slight irritation of the eyes, nose, and throat and possibly a slight decrease in nasal-mucus flow. As yet there is no evidence of a population threshold for the irritant effects of formaldehyde in humans.

Although the Committee recognizes that the general population may react with greater frequency and severity to similar concentrations of formaldehyde than the test populations, no realistic estimate of the magnitude of this effect is possible on the basis of the available data. The studies of public exposure to formaldehyde in indoor air suggest a wide range of sensitivity, with effects reported at 0.01-31.7 ppm. However, these studies were limited in scope, in that the subjects selected were only those who had reported responses to formaldehyde. Data were not available on the proportion of the total exposed population that this group might represent. Although irritation appears to be the most sensitive response, identification of the toxicologic reaction of greatest concern must await the conclusion of ongoing and planned studies.

The preliminary results of an ongoing carcinogenicity study in rodents, the uncertainty about the variability of responses to formaldehyde in normal populations and in hypersensitive groups, and the current inadequacy of data (which leave unresolved the no-observed-effect dose in humans) all point to the advisability of maintaining formaldehyde at the _lowest practical concentration_ to minimize adverse effects on public health. The Committee recognizes that the selection of a lowest practical concentration by CPSC must include consideration of such factors as acceptable degrees of risk and response, economic impacts, sensitivity of analytical methods, and background outdoor-air concentrations.

There is need for a research program to resolve certain questions of health effects from airborne formaldehyde at low concentrations. Such research as identified by the Committee includes:

o the significance of hyperplasia and metaplasia from exposure to nasal irritants in relation to tumor development. The Committee suggests that the nasal epithelium of persons known to be frequently exposed to formaldehyde be examined, to determine whether such individuals have developed lesions similar to those observed in the upper respiratory tract and nasal passages of animals.

o development of quantitative information on the extent of the population that has a marked sensitivity to formaldehyde and the extent of that sensitivity and investigations to ascertain why this group has an increased sensitivity. A double-blind study in persons exposed to formaldehyde for short periods is needed, to explore the range of sensitivity to the irritating effect of formaldehyde at several concentrations below 1 ppm.

o further investigations on possibly susceptible members of the population, such as infants, the elderly, and those with respiratory diseases or other chronic illnesses, to ascertain whether they are indeed more susceptible. This information will be extremely useful in the development of a public indoor-air quality standard. A means for identifying those individuals who may be at higher risk is also needed.

o acquisition of exposure data from extensive epidemiologic studies on select occupational and environmental cohorts, to identify the health effect associated with exposure and to assess the overall health risk associated with a given degree of formaldehyde exposure.

o an evaluation of the human risks associated with dermal exposure to formaldehyde. The steps of percutaneous penetration have not been identified in animals or man. Epidemiologic studies are also not available.

o studies on the effects of formaldehyde on the defense mechanisms and physiology of the respiratory tract and the potential human-health implications of such effects. Disturbance of normal defense mechanisms might make individuals more susceptible to disease from air pollutants and other kinds of respiratory stress.

o investigation of the mechanisms of action of formaldehyde, including its ability to produce sensitization of the airways or other tissues.

o pharmacokinetic studies in animals and comparison with similar data in man, including a study of the movement of formaldehyde across membranes. These studies should also evaluate the importance of the metabolic products of formaldehyde with respect to its toxicity.

o effects of prolonged continuous exposures of various animal species to airborne formaldehyde at low concentrations. The reproductive and teratogenic effects of formaldehyde also need further investigations.

o the importance of possible interactions between formaldehyde and other air pollutants, with emphasis on the likelihood of such reactions at the pollutant concentrations likely to occur in indoor, outdoor, and workplace air.

o   an analysis of the atmospheric fate of formaldehyde in indoor air, including decay rates and effects of such variables as temperature and humidity.

o   an analysis of sources of formaldehyde other than urea-formaldehyde resins that contribute to the overall formaldehyde burden in indoor air.

Table 1. Summary of Selected Animal Acute-Inhalation Data on Formaldehyde

Species	Concentration, ppm	Duration of Exposure	Effects	Reference
Rat	820	0.5 h	LC_{50} (over 3 wks)	Skog, 1950
	482	4 h	LC_{50} (approx.)	Nagornyi et al., 1979
	250	4 h	Death in 2-4 of 6	Carpenter et al., 1949
Cat	650-1,600	8 & 4 h	Death, pulmonary edema, emphysema	Iwanoff, 1911
	735	2 h	Death	Iwanoff, 1911
	650	4 h	Irritation, recovery in 6 d	Iwanoff, 1911
	300	3.5 h	Irritation, recovery in hours	Iwanoff, 1911
Guinea pig	0.3-50	1 h	Increased airway resistance, decreased lung compliance	Amdur, 1960
Mouse	414	4 h	LC_{50}	Nagornyi, et al., 1979
	3.1	10 min	RD_{50}	Kane and Alarie, 1977

Table 2. Summary of Effects of Prolonged Exposure to Formaldehyde in Animals

Concentration, ppm	Duration of Exposure	Species	Effects	Reference
41.5, 83	1 h/d, 3 d/wk x 35 wk	Mouse	Hyperplasia and metaplasia of the tracheal epithelium	Horton et al, 1963
50	5 h/d, 1 d/wk x 18 mo	Hamster	Squamous cell metaplasia	Nettesheim, 1976
15*	6 h/d, 5 d/wk lifetime	Rat	Squamous cell carcinomas in the naso-maxillary epithelium, epithelial dysplasia and squamous cell metaplasia of nasal turbinates	CIIT, 1979b; CIIT, 1980
15*	6 h/d, 5 d/wk lifetime	Mouse	None to date	CIIT, 1979b; CIIT, 1980
12.7	6 h/d, 5 d/wk x 13 wk	Mouse, rat	Nasal irritation, decreased body weight	Battelle Columbus Laboratories, 1977a
10	5 h/d, 5 d/wk x 18 mo	Hamster	Cell proliferation, hyperplasia	Nettesheim, 1976
8	60 d	Rat	Respiratory tract and eye irritation, decreased body weight, decreased number of alveolar macrophages	Dubreuil et al., 1976
6*	6 h/d, 5 d/wk lifetime	Rat	Squamous cell carcinoma of skin in 1 rat, epithelial dysplasia and squamous cell metaplasia of nasal turbinates	CIIT, 1979b; CIIT, 1980
6*	6 h/d, 5 d/wk lifetime	Mouse	None to date	CIIT, 1979b; CIIT, 1980
4.6	45 d	Rat	Yellowing of body hair, decreased body weight	Dubreuil et al., 1976
4	6 h/d, 5 d/wk x 13 wk	Mouse, rat	None observed	Battelle Columbus Laboratories, 1977a

Table 2. (continued)

Concentration, ppm	Duration of Exposure	Species	Effects	Reference
3.8	90 d	Rat, rabbit, dog, monkey, guinea pig	1 of 15 rats died, some inflammation of lungs in all species	Coon et al., 1970
2.4	90 d	Rat	Peribronchial and perivascular hyperemia	Fel'dman and Bonashevskaya, 1971
2*	6 h/d, 5 d/wk lifetime	Rat	Epithelial dysplasia and squamous cell metaplasia of the nasal turbinates	CIIT, 1979b, CIIT, 1980
2*	6 h/d, 5 d/wk lifetime	Mouse	None to date	CIIT, 1979b, CIIT, 1980
1.6	90 d	Rat	Yellowing of body hair	Dubreuil et al., 1976
0.82	90 d	Rat	Peribronchial and perivascular hyperemia	Fel'dman and Bonashevskaya, 1971
0.028	90 d	Rat	None observed	Fel'dman and Bonashevskaya, 1971
0.0098	90 d	Rat	None observed	Fel'dman and Bonashevskaya, 1971

*Study in progress; only interim findings have been reported.

Table 5. Summary of human inhalation data on formaldehyde.

Concentration, ppm	Exposure	Effects	Reference
20	Chamber (< 1 min)	Discomfort, lacrimation	Barnes and Speicher, 1942
13.8	Chamber (30 min)	Eye and nose irritation	Sim and Pattle, 1957
0.5-10	Indoor residential air	Eye irritation, headaches, GI tract symptoms, skin problems, respiratory complaints	Sardinas et al., 1979
4-5	Occupational (10-30 min)	Irritation, discomfort, lacrimation	Fassett, 1963
0.67-4.82	Indoor residential air (infants)	Vomiting, diarrhea, lacrimation	Wisconsin Division of Health, 1978
0.02-4.15	Indoor residential air	Eye and upper respiratory tract irritation, headache, tiredness, nausea, diarrhea	Wisconsin Division of Health, 1978
0.9-2.7	Occupational	Upper respiratory tract irritation, lacrimation	Blejer and Miller, 1966
0.3-2.7	Occupational	Annoying odor, lacrimation, irritation of respiratory tract, disturbed sleep	Shipkovitz, 1968
0.03-2.5	Indoor residential air	Drowsiness, nausea, headache, nose and respiratory tract irritation	Breysse, 1977

Table 3. (continued)

Concentration, ppm	Exposure	Effects	Reference
0.9-1.6	Occupational	Intense eye irritation and itching; dry, sore throat; increased thirst; disturbed sleep	Morrill, 1961
0.25-1.39	Occupational	Upper respiratory tract irritation, coughing, headaches	Kerfoot and Mooney, 1975
0.4-0.8	Occupational	Lowered $FEV_{1.0}/FVC$, upper respiratory tract irritation	Shoenberg and Mitchell, 1975
0.13-0.45	Occupational	Burning and stinging of eyes, nose, and throat; headache	Bourne and Seferian, 1959

Table 4. Summary of Clinical Studies with Formaldehyde

Concentration, ppm	Duration of Exposure	No. Subjects	% of Subjects Responding	Effects	Reference
0.03-3.2*	35 min	33	45 36 19	No significant change in eye blinking rate Doubling of eye blinking rate Increases in eye blinking rate	b
0.03-2.1*	20 min	33	33 20 10 7	Doubling of eye blinking rate "Desire to leave the room" Medium eye irritation Strong odor, strong eye irritation	b
1.6	5 h/d x 4 d	16	94	"Slight discomfort," conjunctival irritation, dryness of nose and throat	a
0.83	5 h/d x 4 d	16	94	"Slight discomfort," conjunctival irritation, dryness of nose and throat	a
0.03-0.5*	5 min	33	11 3 2	Doubling of eye blinking rate "Desire to leave the room" Medium eye irritation	b
0.42	5 h/d x 4 d	16	31	"Slight discomfort," conjunctival irritation, dryness of nose and throat	a
0.25	5 h/d x 4 d	16	19	"Slight discomfort," conjunctival irritation, dryness of nose and throat	a

*Total exposure for 35 min at concentrations increasing from 0.03 to 3.2 ppm.

[a] Andersen, 1979

[b] Weber-Tschopp et al., 1977

Table 5. Summary of Irritation Thresholds[a] (33 Subjects Exposed to Formaldehyde at 0.3-3.2 ppm for 35 min)

Response	Threshold Concentration
Throat irritation	2.1 ppm
Eye blinking rate	1.7 ppm
Eye irritation	1.2 ppm
Nose irritation	1.2 ppm
"Desire to leave the room"	1.2 ppm

[a]Weber-Tschopp et al., 1977

Method	Minimal Detectable Concentration, μg/ml	Estimated Minimal Detectable Concentration,[e] ppm	λ max, nm	Interferences
Chromotropic acid	0.1	0.04	580	NO_2, alkenes, acrolein, acetaldehyde, phenol
Chromotropic acid	0.1	0.01	580	NO_2, alkenes, acrolein, acetaldehyde, phenol
Pararosaniline	0.1	0.06	570	Virtually specific
Pararosaniline	0.1	0.06	560	Virtually specific
Phenylhydrazine	1.0	0.10	520	Color not stable
J-acid[c]	0.03	0.006	468	Formaldehyde precursors
J-acid (fluorescence)	0.001	0.0002	470 (excite) 520 (emission)	Formaldehyde precursors, acrolein
Phenyl-J-acid	0.5	0.10	660	Formaldehyde precursors
p-Phenylenediamine	1.0	0.10	485	SO_2, aliphatic aldehydes
Tryptophan	0.05	0.015	575	Virtually specific
MBTH[b]	0.05	0.03	628	Higher aliphatic aldehydes
Purpald[d]	0.2	0.04	549	Higher aldehydes

[a] Adapted from NRC [1980].
[b] MBTH: 3-methyl-2-benzothiazolone hydrazone
[c] J-acid: 7-amino-4-hydroxy-2-naphthalenesulfonic acid
[d] Purpald: 4-amino-3-hydrazino-5-mercapto-1,2,4-triazole
[e] Based on sampling at 1 L/min for 1 h, and recording a 0.05 absorbance unit difference between blank and sample

Table 7. Recommended and Promulgated Formaldehyde Exposure Limits

Type of Exposure	Country	Exposure Limit, ppm	Status	Reference
Outdoor Ambient Air	United States	0.1 – Ceiling	Recommended (AIHA)	b
	West Germany	0.025 – Ceiling	Promulgated	a
	USSR	0.008 – Ceiling	Promulgated	a
Indoor Air	Denmark	0.12 – Ceiling	Recommended	b
	Netherlands	0.1 – Ceiling	Promulgated	b
	Sweden	0.1–0.4 – Ceiling	Recommended	b
	West Germany	0.1 – Ceiling	Recommended	b
Occupational Air	United States	3.0 – TWA*	Promulgated (OSHA)	b
		2.0 – Ceiling	Promulgated (ACGIH)	b
		1.0 – Ceiling	Recommended (NIOSH)	c
	Denmark	1.0 – TWA	Promulgated	b
	West Germany	1.0 – TWA	Promulgated	d
	East Germany	1.7 – TWA	Promulgated	d
	Sweden	2.5 – Ceiling	Promulgated	d
	Czechoslovakia	1.7 – TWA	Promulgated	d
	USSR	0.4 – Ceiling	Promulgated	d
	Bulgaria	4.0 – Ceiling	Promulgated	c
	Finland	5.0 – Ceiling	Promulgated	c
	Great Britain	10.0 – Ceiling	Promulgated	c
	Hungary	0.8 – Ceiling	Promulgated	c
	Italy	4.7 – Ceiling	Promulgated	c
	Poland	4.7 – Ceiling	Promulgated	c
	Rumania	2.5 – Ceiling	Promulgated	c
	Japan	5.0 – Ceiling	Promulgated	c

*TWA = 8-h time-weighted average
[a]Andersen et al., 1975
[b]Hollowell et al., 1979b
[c]USDHEW, 1976a
[d]Winell, 1975

Table 8. Predicted Irritation Responses of Humans Exposed to Airborne Formaldehyde

Concentration, ppm	% of Population Giving Indicated Response	Degree of Irritation*
1.5-3.0	20	7-10
	>30	5-7
0.5-1.5	10-20	5-7
	>30	3-5
0.25-0.5	20	3-5
<0.25	<20	1-3

*Irritation Index (scale derived from clinical effects noted in the literature)

10 – Strong eye, nose, and throat irritation; great discomfort; strong odor

7 – Moderate eye, nose, and throat irritation; discomfort

5 – Mild eye, nose, and throat irritation; mild discomfort

3 – Slight eye, nose, and throat irritation; slight discomfort

1 – Minimal eye, nose, and throat irritation; minimal discomfort

0 – No effects

REFERENCES

Akabane, J. 1970. Aldehydes and Related Compounds. Int. Encycl. Pharmacol. Ther., Section 20, vol. 2:523-560.

Altshuller, A.P., Cohen, I.R., Meyer, M.E., and Wartburg, A.F., Jr. 1961. Analysis of aliphatic aldehydes in source effluents and in the atmosphere. Anal. Chim. Acta 25:101-117.

Altshuller, A.P., and McPherson, S.P. 1963. Spectrophotometric analysis of aldehydes in the Los Angeles atmosphere. J. Air Pollut. Control. Assoc. 13:109-111. [Chem. Abs. 59:3253d, 1963].

Amdur, M.O. 1960. The response of guinea pigs to inhalation of formaldehyde and formic acid alone and with a sodium chloride aerosol. Int. J. Air Pollut. 3:201-220.

American Conference of Governmental Industrial Hygienists. 1972. TLVs® Threshold Limit Values for Chemical Substances and Physical Agents in the Workroom Environment with Intended Changes for 1972. Cincinnati. 94 p.

American Conference of Governmental Industrial Hygienists. 1974. Documentation of the Threshold Limit Values for Substances in Workroom Air. 3rd ed., 2nd printing. Cincinnati. 352 p.

American Industrial Hygiene Association. 1968. Community Air Quality Guides: Aldehydes. Am. Ind. Hyg. Assoc. J. 29:505-512.

American Public Health Association Intersociety Committee. 1972. Methods of Air Sampling and Analysis. Washington, D.C. 480 p.

Andersen, I. 1979. Formaldehyde in the indoor environment-health implications and the setting of standards. IN Fanger, P.O., and Valbjorn. O;, eds. Indoor Climate; Effects on Human Comfort, Performance and Health in Residential, Commercial, and Light-Industry Buildings. Proc. of the First Internatl. Indoor Climate Symposium, Copenhagen, August 30 - September 1, 1978. Copenhagen: Danish Building Research Institute. p. 65-77. Discussion, p. 77-87.

Andersen, I., Lundqvist, G.R., and Molhave, L. 1975. Indoor air pollution due to chipboard used as a construction material. Atmos. Environ. 9:1121-1127.

Auerbach, C., Moutschen-Dahmen, M., and Moutschen, J. 1977. Genetic and cytogenetical effects of formaldehyde and related compounds. Mutat. Res. 39:317-362.

Barnes, E.C., and Speicher, H.W. 1942. The determination of formaldehyde in air. J. Ind. Hyg. Toxicol. 24:10-17.

Battelle Columbus Laboratories, Columbus, Ohio. 1977a. A ninety day inhalation toxicology study in F-344 albino rats and $B_6C_3F_{16}$ mice exposed to atmospheric formaldehyde vapor. [206] p. Study performed for the Chemical Industry Institute of Toxicology, Research Triangle Park, N.C.

Battelle Columbus Laboratories, Columbus, Ohio. 1977b. Health Effects of Formaldehyde. Final report to National Particleboard Association.

Bilimoria, M.H. 1975. The detection of mutagenic activity of chemicals and tobacco smoke in a bacterial system. Mutat. Res. 31:328. Abstract #39.

Blejer, H.P., and Miller, B.H. 1966. Occupational health report of formaldehyde concentrations and effects on workers at the Bayly Manufacturing Company, Visalia, Calif. Study report number S-1806. Los Angeles, State of California Health and Welfare Agency, Dept. of Public Health, Bureau of Occupational Health.

Bohmer, K. 1934. Formalin poisoning. Dtsche. Z. Gesamte Gerichtl. Med. 23:7-18 [Chem. Abs. 28:5884$_9$, 1934].

Bonashevskaya, T.I. 1973. Amygdaloid lesions after exposure to formaldehdye. Arkh. Anat. Gistol. Embriol. 65(12):56-59. [Chem. Abs. 80:141625w, 1974].

Bourne, H.G., Jr., and Seferian, S. 1959. Formaldehyde in wrinkle-proof apparel produces . . . tears for milady. Ind. Med. Surg. 28:232-233.

Breysse, P.A. 1977. Formaldehyde in mobile and conventional homes. Environ. Health Saf. News 26(1-6). [20] p.

Buss, J., Kuschinsky, K., Kewitz, H., and Koransky, W. 1964. Enterale Resorption von Formaldehyd. Naunyn-Schmiedebergs Archiv. Exp. Pathol. Pharmakol. 247:380-381.

Carpenter, C.P., and Smyth, H.F., Jr. 1946. Chemical burns of the rabbit cornea. Am. J. Ophthalmol. 29:1363-1372.

Carpenter, C.P., Smyth, H.F., Jr., and Pozzani, U.C. 1949. The assay of acute vapor toxicity, and the grading and interpretation of results on 96 chemical compounds. J. Ind. Hyg. Toxicol. 31:343-346.

Chanet, R., Izard, C., and Moustacchi, E. 1975. Genetic effects of formaldehyde in yeast. I. Influence of the growth stages on killing and recombination. Mutat. Res. 33:179-186.

Chemical Industry Institute of Toxicology, Research Triangle Park, N.C. 1979a. Formaldehyde. CIIT Current Status Reports No. 3.

Chemical Industry Institute of Toxicology, Research Triangle Park, N.C. 1979b. Statement concerning research findings. 2 p.

Chemical Industry Institute of Toxicology, Research Triangle Park, N.C. 1980. Progress report on CIIT formaldehyde studies. 2 p.

Clive, D., and Spector, J.F.S. 1975. Laboratory procedure for assessing specific locus mutations at the TK locus in cultured L5178Y mouse lymphoma cells. Mutat. Res. 31:17-29.

Colburn, C.W. 1970. Skin primary irritation and sensitization test on guinea pigs. E.I. duPont de Nemours & Co., Haskell Laboratory for Toxicology and Industrial Medicine, Wilmington, Del.

Coon, R.A., Jones, R.A., Jenkins, L.J., Jr., and Siegel, J. 1970. Animal inhalation studies on ammonia, ethylene glycol, formaldehyde, dimethylamine, and ethanol. Toxicol. Appl. Pharmacol. 16:646-655.

Cralley, L.V. 1942. The effect of irritant gases upon the rate of ciliary activity. J. Ind. Hyg. Toxicol. 24:193-198.

Dalhamn, T., and Rosengren, A. 1971. Effect of different aldehydes on tracheal mucosa. Arch. Otolaryngol. 93:496-500.

Della Porta, G., Colnaghi, M.I. and Parmiani, G. 1968. Non-carcinogenicity of hexamethylenetetramine in mice and rats. Food Cosmet. Toxicol. 6:707-715.

Dubreuil, A., Bouley, G., Godin, J., and Boudene, Cl. 1976. Inhalation, en continu, de faibles doses de formaldehyde: Etude experimentale chez le rat. J. Eur. Toxicol. 9:245-250.

Egle, J.L., Jr. 1972. Retention of inhaled formaldehyde, propionaldehyde, and acrolein in the dog. Arch. Environ. Health 25:119-124.

Ehrenberg, L., Gustafsson, A., and Lundqvist, U. 1956. Chemically induced mutation and sterility in barley. Acta Chem. Scand. 10:492-494.

Engel, H.O., and Calnan, C.D. 1966. Resin dermatitis in a car factory. Br. J. Ind. Med. 23:62-66.

Englesberg, E. 1952. The mutagenic action of formaldehyde on bacteria. J. Bacteriol. 63:1-11.

Epstein, E., and Maibach, H.I. 1966. Formaldehyde allergy; Incidence and patch test problems. Arch. Dermatol. 94:186-190.

Epstein, S.S., Arnold, E., Andrea, J., Bass, W., and Bishop, Y. 1972. Detection of chemical mutagens by the dominant lethal assay in the mouse. Toxicol. Appl. Pharmacol. 23:288-325.

Ettinger, I., and Jeremias, M. 1955. A study of the health hazards involved in working with flameproofed fabrics. New York State Dept. Labor., Div. Ind. Hyg., Mon. Rev. 34:25-27.

Fassett, D.W. 1963. Aldehydes and Acetals. IN Patty, F.A., ed. Industrial Hygiene and Toxicology. 2nd rev. ed. Vol. II. New York: Interscience. p. 1959-1989.

Fel'dman, Yu.G., and Bonashevskaya, T.I. 1971. On the effects of low concentrations of formaldehyde. Hyg. Sanit. (USSR) 36(5):174-180.

Fisher, A.A., Kanof, N.B., and Biondi, E.M. 1962. Free formaldehyde in textiles and paper: Clinical significance. Arch. Dermatol. 86:753-756.

Gamble, J.F., McMichael, A.J., Williams, T., and Battigelli, M. 1976. Respiratory function and symptoms: An environmental-epidemiological study of rubber workers exposed to a phenol-formaldehyde type resin. Am. Ind. Hyg. Assoc. J. 37:499-513.

Glass, W.I. 1961. An outbreak of formaldehyde dermatitis. N.Z. Med. J.

60:423-427. [Cumulated Index Medicus 3:A-534, 1962].

Gofmekler, V.A. 1968. Effect on embryonic development of benzene and formaldehyde in inhalation experiments. Hyg. Sanit. (USSR) 33(3):327-332.

Gosser, L.B., and Butterworth, B.E. 1977. Mutagenicity evaluation of formaldehyde in the L5178Y mouse lymphoma assay. E.I. duPont de Nemours & Co., Haskell Laboratory for Toxicology and Industrial Medicine, Wilmington, Del.

Grant, W.M. 1974. Toxicology of the Eye, 2nd ed. Springfield, Ill.: Charles C Thomas. 1201 p.

Grossman, L.I. 1978. Paresthesia from N2 or N2 substitute; Report of a case. Oral Surg., Oral Med., Oral Pathol. 45:114-115.

Guseva, V.A. 1972. Gonadotropic effect of formaldehyde on male rats during its simultaneous introduction with air and water. Gig. Sanit., No. 10:102-103 [Chem. Abs. 78:80466e, 1973].

Heling, B., Ram, Z., and Heling, I. 1977. The root treatment of teeth with Toxavit; Report of a case. Oral Surg., Oral Med., Oral Pathol. 43:306-309.

Helwig, H. 1977. [How harmless is formaldehyde? (letter)] Dtsch. Med. Wochenschr. 102:1612-1613. [Cumulated Index Medicus 19:2459, 1978].

Hollowell, C.D., Berk, J.V., Lin, C-I., and Turiel, I. 1979a. Indoor air quality in energy-efficient buildings. Lawrence Berkeley Laboratory, Energy and Environment Division, University of California/Berkeley. [Report No.] LBL-8892, EEB Vent 79-2. 12 p.

Hollowell, C.D., Berk, J.V., and Traynor, G.W. 1979b. Impact of reduced infiltration and ventilation on indoor air quality in residential buildings. ASHRAE Trans. 85, Part 1:816-826, Discussion p. 827.

Horton, A.V., Tye, R., and Stemmer, K.L. 1963. Experimental carcinogenesis of the lung. Inhalation of gaseous formaldehyde or an aerosol of coal tar by C3H mice. J. Natl. Cancer Inst. 30:31-43.

Hsie, A.W., O'Neill, J.P., San Sebastian, J.R., Couch, D.B., Fuscoe, J.C., Sun, W.N.C., Brimer, P.A., Machanoff, R., Riddle, J.C., Forbes, N.L., and Hsie, M.H. 1978. Mutagenicity of carcinogens: Study of 101 agents in a quantitative mammalian cell mutation system, CHO/HGPRT. Fed. Proc. Fed. Am. Soc. Exp. Biol. 37:1384. Abstract #633.

Hurni, H. and Ohder, H. 1973. Reproduction study with formaldehyde and hexamethylenetetramine in beagle dogs. Food Cosmet. Toxicol. 11:459-462.

Iwanoff, N. 1911. Experimentelle Studien uber den Einfluss technisch und hygienisch wichtiger Gase und Dampfe auf den Organismus. Teil XVI, XVII, XVIII: Uber einige praktisch wichtige Aldehyde (Formaldehyd, Acetaldehyd, Akrolein). Arch. Hyg. 73:307-340.

Jordan, W.P., Jr., Sherman, W.T., and King, S.E. 1979. Threshold responses in formaldehyde-sensitive subjects. J. Am. Acad. Dermatol. 1:44-48.

Kane, L.E., and Alarie, Y. 1977. Sensory irritation to formaldehyde and acrolein during single and repeated exposures in mice. Am. Ind. Hyg. Assoc. J. 38:509-522.

Kane, L.E., Barrow, C.S., and Alarie, Y. 1979. A short-term test to predict acceptable levels of exposure to airborne sensory irritants. Am. Ind. Hyg. Assoc. J. 40:207-229.

Kensler, C.J., and Battista, S.P. 1963. Components of cigarette smoke with ciliary-depressant activity; Their selective removal by filters containing activated charcoal granules. N. Engl. J. Med. 269:1161-1166.

Kerfoot, E.J., and Mooney, T.F., Jr. 1975. Formaldehyde and paraformaldehyde study in funeral homes. Am. Ind. Hyg. Assoc. J. 36:533-537.

Kitchens, J.F., Casner, R.E., Edwards, G.S., Harward, W.E., III., and Macri, B.J. 1976. Investigation of selected potential environmental contaminants: Formaldehyde. Final technical report. Atlantic Research Corp., Alexandria, Va. Rept. no. ARC 49-5681. EPA/560/2-76/009. 217 p.

Klecak, G. 1977. Indentification of contact allergens: Predictive tests in animals. IN Marzulli, F.N., and Maibach, H.I., eds. Advances in Modern Toxicology, vol. 4. Dermatotoxicology and Pharmacology. Washington, D.C.: Hemisphere Publishing. p. 305-339.

Kline, B.S. 1925. Formaldehyd poisoning; With report of a fatal case. Arch. Intern. Med. 36:220-228.

Koops, A., and Butterworth, B.E. 1976. In vitro microbial mutagenicity studies of formaldehyde. E.I. duPont de Nemours & Co., Haskell Laboratory for Toxicology and Industrial Medicine, Wilmington, Del.

Kulle, T.J., and Cooper G.P. 1975. Effects of formaldehyde and ozone on the trigeminal nasal sensory system. Arch. Environ. Health 30:237-243.

Kuschner, M., Laskin, S., Drew, R.T., Cappiello, V., and Nelson, N. 1975. Inhalation carcinogenicity of alpha halo ethers. III. Lifetime and limited period inhalation studies with bis(chloromethyl)ether at 0.1 ppm. Arch. Environ. Health 30:73-77.

Lazar, P. 1966. Reactions to nail hardeners. Arch. Dermatol. 94:446-448.

Logan, W.S., and Perry, H.O. 1973. Contact dermatitis to resin-containing casts. Clin. Orthop. Relat. Res., No. 90:150-152.

Loomis, T.A. 1979. Formaldehyde toxicity. Arch. Pathol. Lab. Med. 103:321-324.

Magnusson, B., and Kligman, A.M. 1977. Usefulness of guinea pigs tests for detection of contact sensitizers. IN Marzulli, F.N., and H.I. Maibach, eds. Advances in Modern Toxicology, vol. 4. Dermatotoxicology and Pharmacology. Washington, D.C.: Hemisphere Publishing p. 551-560.

Maibach, H. 1978. Reliable animal test for predicting human skin sensitizers. U.S. Consumer Product Safety Commission. Contract CPSC-C-77-0087.

Maibach, H.I., and Franz T. [1980]. Provocative use tests with formalin: Dose response relationships. Submitted for publication.

Manna, G.K., and Parida, B.B. 1967. Formalin-induced sex chromosome breakage in the spermatocyte cells of the grasshopper, Tristria pulvinata. J. Cytol. Genet. 1:88-91.

Marzulli, F.N., and Maibach, H.I. 1973. Antimicrobials: Experimental contact sensitization in man. J. Soc. Cosmet. Chem. 24:399-421. [Chem. Abs. 80:56181d, 1974].

Marzulli, F.N., and Maibach, H.I. 1977. Contact allergy: Predictive testing in humans. IN Marzulli, F.N., and H.I. Maibach, eds. Advances in Modern Toxicology, vol. 4. Dermatotoxicology and Pharmacology. Washington, D.C.: Hemisphere Publishing. p. 353-372.

Miksch, R.R., Anthon, D.W., Fanning, L.Z., Revzan, K., Glanville, J., and Hollowell, C.D. [1980]. A modified pararosaniline method for the determination of formaldehyde in air. Publication in progress.

Monsanto Company, St. Louis, Missouri. 1973a. Ninety-day rat feeding study on formaldehyde. Study performed by Pharmacopathics Research Laboratories, Inc., Laurel, Md. Project No. PRL 73-13.

Monsanto Company, St. Louis, Missouri. 1973b. Ninety-day dog feeding study on formaldehyde. Study performed by Pharmacopathics Research Laboratories, Inc., Laurel, Md. Project No. PRL 73-14.

Montgomery, S. 1976. Paresthesia following endodontic treatment. J. Endodontics 2:345-347.

Morrill, E.E., Jr. 1961. Formaldehyde exposure from paper process solved by air sampling and current studies. Air Cond. Heat. Vent. 58(7):94-95.

Nagornyi, P.A., Sudakova, Zh.A., and Shchablenko, S.M. 1979. General toxic and allergic effects of formaldehyde. Gig. Tr. Prof. Zabol. No. 1:27-30. [Chem. Abs. 90:133606g, 1979].

National Research Council, Committee on Aldehydes. [1980]. Formaldehyde and other Selected Aldehydes. Washington, D.C.: National Academy of Sciences. [In preparation].

Natvig, H., Andersen, J., and Wulff Rasmussen, E. 1971. A contribution to the toxicological evaluation of hexamethylenetetramine. Food Cosmet. Toxicol. 9:491-500.

Neely, W.B. 1964. The metabolic fate of formaldehyde-^{14}C intraperitoneally administered to the rat. Biochem. Pharmacol. 13:1137-1142.

Nettesheim, P. 1976. [Unpublished data]. Oak Ridge National Laboratory, Tenn.

North American Contact Dermatitis Group. 1973. Epidemiology of contact dermatitis in North America: 1972. Arch. Dermatol. 108:537-540.

Occupational Safety and Health Administration. 1979. Air contaminants. 29 CFR 1910:1000.

Odom, R.B., and Maibach, H.I. 1977. Contact urticaria: A different contact dermatitis. IN Marzulli, F.N., and Maibach, H.I., eds. Advances in Modern Toxicology, vol. 4. Dermatotoxicology and Pharmacology. Washington, D.C.: Hemisphere Publishing. p. 441-453.

O'Quinn, S.E., and Kennedy, C.B. 1965. Contact dermatitis due to formaldehyde in clothing textiles. J. Am Med. Assoc. 194:593-596.

Orringer, E.P., and Mattern, W.D. 1976. Formaldehyde-induced hemolysis during chronic hemodialysis. N. Engl. J. Med. 294:1416-1420.

Pirila, V., and Kilpio, O. 1949. On dermatitis caused by formaldehyde and its compounds. Ann. Med. Intern. Fenn. 38:38-51. [Qtly. Cumulative Index Medicus 46:1129, 1949].

Porter, J.A.H. 1975. Acute respiratory distress following formalin inhalation. Lancet 2:603-604.

Potts, A.M., Praglin J., Farkas I., Orbison, L., and Chickering, D. 1955. Studies on the visual toxicity of methanol. VIII. Additional observations on methanol poisoning in the primate test object. Am. J. Ophthalmol. 40(5, Pt. II):76-83.

Rapoport, I.A. 1948. Mutations under the influence of unsaturated aldehydes. Dokl. Akad. Nauk SSSR 61:713-715. [Chem. Abs. 43:1115i, 1949].

Rostenberg, A., Jr., Bairstow, B., and Luther, T.W. 1952. A study of eczematous sensitivity to formaldehyde. J. Invest. Dermatol. 19:459-462.

Rudner, E.J., Clendenning, W.E., Epstein, E., Fisher, A.A., Jillson, O.F., Jordan, W.P., Kanof, N., Larsen, W., Maibach, H., Mitchell, J.C, O'Quinn, S.E., Schorr, W.F., and Sulzberger, M.B. 1973. Epidemiology of contact dermatitis in North America. Arch. Dermatol. 108:537-540.

Rumack, B.H. 1978. Position paper: Urea-formaldehyde foam. Rocky Mountain Poison Center, Denver, Colorado [30] p.

Rusch, G.M., Sellekumar, A.R., LaMendola, S.L., Katz, G.V., Laskin, S., and Albert, R.E. [1980]. Inhalation studies with combined formaldehyde and hydrogen chloride vapors. [Submitted for publication].

Sardinas, A.V., Most, R.S., Giulietti, M.A., and Honchar, P. 1979. Health effects associated with urea-formaldehyde foam insulation in Connecticut. J. Environ. Health 41:270-272.

Schoenberg, J.B., and Mitchell, C.A. 1975. Airway disease caused by phenolic (phenol-formaldehyde) resin exposure. Arch. Environ. Health 30:574-577.

Schuck, E.A., Stephens, E.R., and Middleton, J.T. 1966. Eye irritation response at low concentrations of irritants. Arch. Environ. Health 13:570-575.

Sheveleva, G.A. 1971. Specific action of formaldehyde on the embryogeny and progeny of rats. Toksikol. Nov. Prom. Khim. Veschestv., No. 12:78-86. [Chem. Abs. 75:139154v, 1971].

Shipkovitz, H.D. 1968. Formaldehyde vapor emissions in the permanent-press fabrics industry. Report No. TR-52. Cincinnati: U.S. Dept. of Health, Education, and Welfare. Public Health Service. Consumer Protection and Environmental Health Service. Environmental Control Administration.

Sim, V.M., and Pattle, R.E. 1957. Effect of possible smog irritants on human subjects. J. Am. Med. Assoc. 165:1908-1913.

Skog, E. 1950. A toxicological investigation of lower aliphatic aldehydes. I. Toxicity of formaldehyde, acetaldehyde, propionaldehyde and butyraldehyde; as well as of acrolein and crotonaldehyde. Acta Pharmacol. Toxicol. 6:299-318.

Smyth, H.F., Jr., Seaton, J., and Fischer, L. 1941. The single dose toxicity of some glycols and derivatives. J. Ind. Hyg. Toxicol. 23:259-268.

Solyanik, R.G., Fedorov, Yu. V., and Rapoport, I.A. 1972. The mutagenic effect of some alkylating compounds on eastern equine encephalomyelitis virus. Sov. Genet. 8:412-413.

Stupfel, M. 1976. Recent advances in investigations of toxicity of automotive exhaust. Environ. Health Perspect. 17:253-285.

Tabershaw, I.R., Doyle, H.N., Gaudette, L., Lamm, S.H., and Wong, O. 1979. A review of the formaldehyde problems in mobile homes. Tabershaw Occupational Medicine Associates, P.A., Rockville, MD. 19 p.

Tephly, T.R., Watkins, W.D., and Goodman, J.I. 1974. The biochemical toxicology of methanol. IN: Hayes, W.J., Jr., ed. Essays in Toxicology, volume 5. New York: Academic Press. p. 149-177.

Tsuchiya, K., Hayashi, Y., Onodera, M., and Hasegawa, T. 1975. Toxicity of formaldehyde in experimental animals--concentrations of the chemical in the elution from dishes of formaldehyde resin and in some vegetables. Keio J. Med. 24:19-37.

U.S. Consumer Product Safety Commission. Ad Hoc Task Force, Epidemiology Study on Formaldehyde. 1979. Epidemiological studies in the context of assessment of the health impact of indoor air pollution. [34] p.

U.S. Consumer Product Safety Commission. Directorate for Hazard Identification and Analysis-Epidemiology. 1978. Summary of In-Depth Investigations, Newspaper Clippings, Consumer Complaints and State Reports, and Incidents Investigated by the Connecticut State Health Department: Urea Formaldehyde Foam Home Insulation. 15 p.

U.S. Department of Health, Education, and Welfare, Public Health Service, Center for Disease Control, National Institute for Occupational Safety and Health. 1976a. Criteria for a Recommended Standard . . . Occupational Exposure to Formaldehyde. Washington, D.C.: Government Printing Office. 165 p.

[DHEW (NIOSH) Publication No. 77-126].

U.S. Department of Health, Education, and Welfare, Public Health Service, Center for Disease Control, National Institute for Occupational Safety and Health. 1976b. Irritant Effects of Industrial Chemicals: Formaldehyde, by Lowell G. Wayne, Robert J. Bryan, and Kenneth Ziedman. Washington, D.C.: Government Printing Office. [138 p.] [DHEW (NIOSH) Publication No. 77-117].

Uotila, L., and Koivusalo, M. 1974. Formaldehyde dehydrogenase from human liver; Purification, properties, and evidence for the formation of glutathione thiol esters by the enzyme. J. Biol. Chem. 249:7653-7663.

Walker, J.F. 1964. Formaldehyde. 3rd ed. New York: Reinhold. 701 p. (American Chemical Society Monograph Series No. 159).

Watanabe, F., Matsunaga, T., Soejima, T., and Iwata, Y. 1954. Study on the carcinogenicity of aldehyde. I. Experimentally produced rat sarcomas by repeated injections of aqueous solution of formaldehyde. Gann 45:451-452. [Current List of Med. Literature 27:32874, 1955].

Weber-Tschopp, A., Fischer, T., and Grandjean, E. 1977. Reizwirkungen des Formaldehyds (HCHO) auf den Menschen. Irritating effects of formaldehyde on men. Int. Arch. Occup. Environ. Health 39:207-218.

Weber-Tschopp, A., Jermini, C., and Grandjean, E. 1976. Air pollution and irritation due to cigaret smoke. Soz. Praeventivmed. 21(2-3):101-106. [Chem. Abs. 86:33655w, 1977].

Weger, A. 1927. Thalamischer Symptomenkomplex bei Formalinintoxikation. Z. Gesamte Neurol. Psychiatr. 111:370-382. [Qtly. Cumulative Index Medicus 3:1113, 1928].

Williams, R.T. 1959. Detoxication Mechanisms: The Metabolism and Detoxication of Drugs, Toxic Substances and Other Organic Compounds, 2nd ed. New York: John Wiley & Sons. p. 88-90.

Winell, M. 1975. An international comparison of hygienic standards for chemicals in the work environment. Ambio 4:34-36.

Wisconsin, Division of Health, Bureau of Prevention, Section of Environmental Epidemiology. 1978. Statistics of particleboard related formaldehdye cases through December 15, 1978. [4] p.

Yefremov, G.G. 1970. State of the upper respiratory tract in formaldehyde production workers (By the data of a special investigation). Zh. Ushn. Nos. Gorl. Bolezn. 30:11-15, Sept-Oct.

Zannini, D., and Russo, L. 1957. [Long-standing lesions in the respiratory tract following acute poisoning with irritating gases.] Lav. Um. 9:241-254.